AF348312

The Children

by

Alice Meynell

The Children
by Alice Meynell

Copyright © 2024

All Rights reserved.

No part of this publication may be reproduced,
stored in a retrieval system, or transmitted in any
form or by any means, electronic, mechanical,
photocopying or Otherwise, without the written
permission of the publisher.
The author/editor asserts the moral right to
be identified as the author/editor of this work.

ISBN: 978-93-67147-19-1

Published by

DOUBLE 9 BOOKS

2/13-B, Ansari Road
Daryaganj, New Delhi – 110002
info@double9books.com
www.double9books.com
Tel. 011-40042856

This book is under public domain

ABOUT THE AUTHOR

Alice Meynell (1847-1922) was a British writer, poet, and editor renowned for her lyrical and introspective prose and poetry. Her work reflects her deep engagement with themes of nature, spirituality, and the human condition. She was born in London, she was educated privately and began writing at an early age. Her background in literature and her exposure to various intellectual circles shaped her literary voice. Notable works of the author are The Rhythm of Life (1903): A collection of essays and poems reflecting on the natural world and spiritual life, Preludes (1885): A collection of her early poems that established her reputation as a poet and The Colour of Life (1897): Another significant collection of her poetry. Meynell's writing is characterized by its lyrical quality, introspective nature, and focus on themes of spirituality and nature. Her poetic style is marked by a delicate and thoughtful approach to language. Meynell's work has influenced subsequent generations of poets and writers. Her exploration of the spiritual and natural worlds, combined with her elegant prose, has left a lasting impact on English literature. Alice Meynell remains a respected figure in literary circles, known for her profound reflections on life and her contributions to poetry and prose.

CONTENTS

RAVELLERS WITH A BIRD, I

To attend to a living child is to be baffled in your humour, disappointed of your pathos, and set freshly free from all the pre-occupations. You cannot anticipate him. Blackbirds, overheard year by year, do not compose the same phrases; never two leitmotifs alike. Not the tone, but the note alters. So with the uncovenated ways of a child you keep no tryst. They meet you at another place, after failing you where you tarried; your former experiences, your documents are at fault. You are the fellow traveller of a bird. The bird alights and escapes out of time to your footing.

No man's fancy could be beforehand, for instance, with a girl of four years old who dictated a letter to a distant cousin, with the sweet and unimaginable message: "I hope you enjoy yourself with your loving dolls." A boy, still younger, persuading his mother to come down from the heights and play with him on the floor, but sensible, perhaps, that there was a dignity to be observed none the less, entreated her, "Mother, do be a lady frog." None ever said their good things before these indeliberate authors. Even their own kind—children—have not preceded them. No child in the past ever found the same replies as the girl of five whose father made that appeal to feeling which is doomed to a different, perverse, and unforeseen success. He was rather tired with writing, and had a mind to snare some of the yet uncaptured flock of her sympathies. "Do you know, I have been working hard, darling? I work to buy things for you." "Do you work," she asked, "to buy the lovely puddin's?" Yes, even for these. The subject must have seemed to her to be worth pursuing. "And do you work to buy the fat? I don't like fat."

The sympathies, nevertheless, are there. The same child was to be soothed at night after a weeping dream that a skater had been drowned in the Kensington Round Pond. It was suggested to her that she should forget it by thinking about the one unfailing and gay subject—her wishes. "Do you know," she said, without loss of time, "what I should like best in all the world? A thundred dolls and a whistle!" Her mother was so overcome by this tremendous numeral, that she could make no offer as to the dolls. But the whistle seemed practicable. "It is for me to whistle for cabs," said the child, with a sudden moderation, "when I go to parties." Another morning she came down radiant, "Did you hear a great noise in the miggle of the night? That was me crying. I cried because I dreamt that Cuckoo [a brother] had swallowed a bead into his nose."

The mere errors of children are unforeseen as nothing is—no, nothing feminine—in this adult world. "I've got a lotter than you," is the word of a very young egotist. An older child says, "I'd better go, bettern't I, mother?" He calls a little space at the back of a London house, "the backy-garden." A little creature proffers almost daily the reminder at luncheon—at tart-time: "Father, I hope you will remember that I am the favourite of the crust." Moreover, if an author set himself to invent the naïf things that children might do in their Christmas plays at home, he would hardly light upon the device of the little *troupe* who, having no footlights, arranged upon the floor a long row of—candle-shades!

"It's *jolly* dull without you, mother," says a little girl who—gentlest of the gentle—has a dramatic sense of slang, of which she makes no secret. But she drops her voice somewhat to disguise her feats of metathesis, about which she has doubts and which are involuntary: the "stand-wash," the "sweeping-crosser," the "sewing chamine." Genoese peasants have the same prank when they try to speak Italian.

Children forget last year so well that if they are Londoners they should by any means have an impression of the country or the sea annually. A London little girl watches a fly upon the wing, follows it with her pointing finger, and names it "bird." Her brother, who wants to play with a bronze Japanese lobster, ask "Will you please let me have that tiger?"

At times children give to a word that slight variety which is the most touching kind of newness. Thus, a child of three asks you to save him. How moving a word, and how freshly said! He had heard of the "saving" of other things of interest—especially chocolate creams taken for safe-keeping—and he asks, "Who is going to save me to-day? Nurse is going out, will you save me, mother?" The same little variant upon common use is in another child's courteous reply to a summons to help in the arrangement of some flowers, "I am quite at your ease."

A child, unconscious little author of things told in this record, was taken lately to see a fellow author of somewhat different standing from her own, inasmuch as he is, among other things, a Saturday Reviewer. As he dwelt in a part of the South-west of the town unknown to her, she noted with interest the shops of the neighbourhood as she went, for they might be those of the *fournisseurs* of her friend. "That is his bread shop, and that is his book shop. And that, mother," she said finally, with even heightened sympathy, pausing before a blooming *parterre* of confectionery hard by the abode of her man of letters, "that, I suppose, is where he buys his sugar pigs."

In all her excursions into streets new to her, this same child is intent upon a certain quest — the quest of a genuine collector. We have all heard of collecting butterflies, of collecting china-dogs, of collecting cocked hats, and so forth; but her pursuit gives her a joy that costs her nothing except a sharp look-out upon the proper names over all shop-windows. No hoard was ever lighter than hers. "I began three weeks ago next Monday, mother," she says with precision, "and I have got thirty-nine." "Thirty-nine what?" "Smiths."

FELLOW TRAVELLERS WITH A BIRD, II

The mere gathering of children's language would be much like collecting together a handful of flowers that should be all unique, single of their kind. In one thing, however, do children agree, and that is the rejection of most of the conventions of the authors who have reported them. They do not, for example, say "me is;" their natural reply to "are you?" is "I are." One child, pronouncing sweetly and neatly, will have nothing but the nominative pronoun. "Lift I up and let I see it raining," she bids; and told that it does not rain, resumes, "Lift I up and let I see it not raining."

An elder child had a rooted dislike to a brown corduroy suit ordered for her by maternal authority. She wore the garments under protest, and with some resentment. At the same time it was evident that she took no pleasure in hearing her praises sweetly sung by a poet, her friend. He had imagined the making of this child in the counsels of Heaven, and the decreeing of her soft skin, of her brilliant eyes, and of her hair—"a brown tress." She had gravely heard the words as "a brown dress," and she silently bore the poet a grudge for having been the accessory of Providence in the mandate that she should wear the loathed corduroy. The unpractised ear played another little girl a like turn. She had a phrase for snubbing any anecdote that sounded improbable. "That," she said more or less after Sterne, "is a cotton-wool story."

The learning of words is, needless to say, continued long after the years of mere learning to speak. The young child now takes a current word into use, a little at random, and now makes a new one, so as to save the interruption of a pause for search. I have certainly detected, in children old enough to show their motives, a conviction that a word of their own making is as good a communication as another, and as intelligible. There is even a general implicit conviction among them that the grown-up people, too, make words by the wayside as occasion befalls. How otherwise should words be so numerous that every day brings forward some hitherto unheard? The child would be surprised to know how irritably poets are refused the faculty and authority which he thinks to belong to the common world.

There is something very cheerful and courageous in the setting-out of a child on a journey of speech with so small baggage and with so much confidence in the chances of the hedge. He goes free, a simple adventurer. Nor does he make any officious effort to invent anything strange or particularly expressive or descriptive. The child trusts genially to his hearer. A very young boy, excited by his first sight of sunflowers, was eager to describe them, and called them, without allowing himself to be checked for the trifle of a name, "summersets." This was simple and unexpected; so was the comment of a sister a very little older. "Why does he call those flowers summersets?" their mother said; and the girl, with a darkly brilliant look of humour and penetration, answered, "because they are so big." There seemed to be no further question possible after an explanation that was presented thus charged with meaning.

To a later phase of life, when a little girl's vocabulary was, somewhat at random, growing larger, belong a few brave phrases hazarded to express a meaning well realized—a personal matter. Questioned as to the eating of an uncertain number of buns just before lunch, the child averred, "I took them just to appetize my hunger." As she betrayed a familiar knowledge of the tariff of an attractive confectioner, she was asked whether she and her sisters had been frequenting those little tables on their way from school. "I sometimes go in there, mother," she confessed; "but I generally speculate outside."

Children sometimes attempt to cap something perfectly funny with something so flat that you are obliged to turn the conversation. Dryden does the same thing, not with jokes, but with his sublimer passages. But sometimes a child's deliberate banter is quite intelligible to elders. Take the letter written by a little girl to a mother who had, it seems, allowed her family to see that she was inclined to be satisfied with something of her own writing. The child has a full and gay sense of the sweetest kinds of irony. There was no need for her to write, she and her mother being both at home, but the words must have seemed to her worthy of a pen:—"My dear mother, I really wonder how you can be proud of that article, if it is worthy to be called a article, which I doubt. Such a unletterary article. I cannot call it letterature. I hope you will not write any more such unconventionan trash."

This is the saying of a little boy who admired his much younger sister, and thought her forward for her age: "I wish people knew just how old she is, mother, then they would know she is onward. They can see she is pretty, but they can't know she is such a onward baby."

Thus speak the naturally unreluctant; but there are other children who in time betray a little consciousness and a slight *méfiance* as to where the adult sense of humour may be lurking in wait for them, obscure. These children may not be shy enough to suffer any self-checking in their talk, but they are now and then to be heard slurring a word of which they do not feel too sure. A little girl whose sensitiveness was barely enough to cause her to stop to choose between two words, was wont to bring a cup of tea to the writing-table of her mother, who had often feigned indignation at the weakness of what her Irish maid always called "the infusion." "I'm afraid it's bosh again, mother," said the child; and then, in a half-whisper, "Is bosh right, or wash, mother?" She was not told, and decided for herself, with doubts, for bosh. The afternoon cup left the kitchen an infusion, and reached the library "bosh" thenceforward.

CHILDREN IN MIDWINTER

Children are so flowerlike that it is always a little fresh surprise to see them blooming in winter. Their tenderness, their down, their colour, their fulness—which is like that of a thick rose or of a tight grape—look out of season. Children in the withering wind are like the soft golden-pink roses that fill the barrows in Oxford Street, breathing a southern calm on the north wind. The child has something better than warmth in the cold, something more subtly out of place and more delicately contrary; and that is coolness. To be cool in the cold is the sign of a vitality quite exquisitely alien from the common conditions of the world. It is to have a naturally, and not an artificially, different and separate climate.

We can all be more or less warm—with fur, with skating, with tea, with fire, and with sleep—in the winter. But the child is fresh in the wind, and wakes cool from his dreams, dewy when there is hoar-frost everywhere else; he is "more lovely and more temperate" than the summer day and than the winter day alike. He overcomes both heat and cold by another climate, which is the climate of life; but that victory of life is more delicate and more surprising in the tyranny of January. By the sight and the touch of children, we are, as it were, indulged with something finer than a fruit or a flower in untimely bloom. The childish bloom is always untimely. The fruit and flower will be common later on; the strawberries will be a matter of course anon, and the asparagus dull in its day. But a child is a perpetual *primeur*.

Or rather he is not in truth always untimely. Some few days in the year are his own season—unnoticed days of March or April, soft, fresh and equal, when the child sleeps and rises with the sun. Then he looks as though he had his brief season, and ceases for a while to seem strange.

It is no wonder that we should try to attribute the times of the year to children; their likeness is so rife among annuals. For man and woman we are naturally accustomed to a longer rhythm; their metre is so obviously their own, and of but a single stanza, without repetition, without renewel, without refrain. But it is by an intelligible illusion that we look for a quick waxing and waning in the lives of young children—for a waxing that shall come again another time, and for a waning that shall not be final, shall not be fatal. But every winter shows us how human they are, and how they are little pilgrims and visitants among the things that look like their kin. For every winter shows them free from the east wind; more perfectly than their elders, they enclose the climate of life. And, moreover, with them the climate of life is the climate of the spring of life; the climate of a human March that is sure to make a constant progress, and of a human April that never hesitates. The child "breathes April and May"—an inner April and his own May.

The winter child looks so much the more beautiful for the season as his most brilliant uncles and aunts look less well. He is tender and gay in the east wind. Now more than ever must the lover beware of making a comparison between the beauty of the admired woman and the beauty of a child. He is indeed too wary ever to make it. So is the poet. As comparisons are necessary to him, he will pay a frankly impossible homage, and compare a woman's face to something too fine, to something it never could emulate. The Elizabethan lyrist is safe among lilies and cherries, roses, pearls, and snow. He undertakes the beautiful office of flattery, and flatters with courage. There is no hidden reproach in the praise. Pearls and snow suffer, in a sham fight, a mimic defeat that does them no harm, and no harm comes to the lady's beauty from a competition so impossible. She never wore a lily or a coral in the colours of her face, and their beauty is not hers. But here is the secret: she is compared with a flower because she could not endure to be compared with a child. That would touch her too nearly. There would be the human texture and the life like hers, but immeasurably more lovely. No colour, no surface, no eyes of woman have ever been comparable with the colour, the surface, and the eyes of childhood. And no poet has ever run the risk of such a defeat. Why, it is defeat enough for a woman to have her face, however well-favoured, close to a child's, even if there is no one by who should be rash enough to approach them still nearer by a comparison.

This, needless to say, is true of no other kind of beauty than that beauty of light, colour, and surface to which the Elizabethans referred, and which suggested their flatteries in disfavour of the lily. There are, indeed, other adult beauties, but those are such as make no allusions to the garden. What is here affirmed is that the beautiful woman who is widely and wisely likened to the flowers, which are inaccessibly more beautiful, must not, for her own sake, be likened to the always accessible child.

Besides light and colour, children have a beauty of finish which is much beyond that of more finished years. This gratuitous addition, this completeness, is one of their unexpected advantages. Their beauty of finish is the peculiarity of their first childhood, and loses, as years are added, that little extra character and that surprise of perfection. A bloom disappears, for instance. In some little children the whole face, and especially all the space between the growth of the eyebrows and the growth of the hair, is covered with hardly perceptible down as soft as bloom. Look then at the eyebrows themselves. Their line is as definite as in later life, but there is in the child the flush given by the exceeding fineness of the delicate hairs. Moreover, what becomes, afterwards, of the length and the curl of the eyelash? What is there in growing up that is destructive of a finish so charming as this?

Queen Elizabeth forbade any light to visit her face "from the right or from the left" when her portrait was a-painting. She was an observant woman, and liked to be lighted from the front. It is a light from the right or from the left that marks an elderly face with minute shadows. And you must place a child in such a light, in order to see the finishing and parting caress that infancy has given to his face. The down will then be found even on the thinnest and clearest skin of the middle red of his cheek. His hair, too, is imponderably fine, and his nails are not much harder than petals.

To return to the child in January. It is his month for the laying up of dreams. No one can tell whether it is so with all children, or even with a majority; but with some children, of passionate fancy, there occurs now and then a children's dance, or a party of any kind, which has a charm and glory mingled with uncertain dreams. Never forgotten, and yet never certainly remembered as a fact of this life, is such an evening. When many and many a later pleasure, about the reality of which there never was any kind of doubt, has been long forgotten, that evening—as to which all is doubt—is impossible to forget. In a few years it has become so remote that the history of Greece derives antiquity from it. In later years it is still doubtful, still a legend.

The child never asked how much was fact. It was always so immeasurably long ago that the sweet party happened—if indeed it happened. It had so long taken its place in that past wherein lurks all the antiquity of the world. No one would know, no one could tell him, precisely what occurred. And who can know whether—if it be indeed a dream—he has dreamt it often, or has dreamt once that he had dreamt it often? That dubious night is entangled in repeated visions during the lonely life a child lives in sleep; it is intricate with illusions. It becomes the most mysterious and the least worldly of all memories, a spiritual past. The word pleasure is too trivial for such a remembrance. A midwinter long gone by contained the suggestion of such dreams; and the midwinter of this year must doubtless be preparing for the heart of many an ardent young child a like legend and a like antiquity. For the old it is a mere present.

THAT PRETTY PERSON

During the many years in which "evolution" was the favourite word, one significant lesson—so it seems—was learnt, which has outlived controversy, and has remained longer than the questions at issue—an interesting and unnoticed thing cast up by the storm of thoughts. This is a disposition, a general consent, to find the use and the value of process, and even to understand a kind of repose in the very wayfaring of progress. With this is a resignation to change, and something more than resignation—a delight in those qualities that could not be but for their transitoriness.

What, then, is this but the admiration, at last confessed by the world, for childhood? Time was when childhood was but borne with, and that for the sake of its mere promise of manhood. We do not now hold, perhaps, that promise so high. Even, nevertheless, if we held it high, we should acknowledge the approach to be a state adorned with its own conditions.

But it was not so once. As the primitive lullaby is nothing but a patient prophecy (the mother's), so was education, some two hundred years ago, nothing but an impatient prophecy (the father's) of the full stature of body and mind. The Indian woman sings of the future hunting. If her song is not restless, it is because she has a sense of the results of time, and has submitted her heart to experience. Childhood is a time of danger; "Would it were done." But, meanwhile, the right thing is to put it to sleep and guard its slumbers. It will pass. She sings prophecies to the child of his hunting, as she sings a song about the robe while she spins, and a song about bread as she grinds corn. She bids good speed.

John Evelyn was equally eager, and not so submissive. His child— "that pretty person" in Jeremy Taylor's letter of condolence—was chiefly precious to him inasmuch as he was, too soon, a likeness of the man he never lived to be. The father, writing with tears when the boy was dead, says of him: "At two and a half years of age he pronounced English, Latin, and French exactly, and could perfectly read in these three languages." As he lived precisely five years, all he did was done at that little age, and it comprised this: "He got by heart almost the entire vocabulary of Latin and French primitives and words, could make congruous syntax, turn English into Latin, and *vice versa*, construe and prove what he read, and did the government and use of relatives, verbs, substantives, ellipses, and many figures and tropes, and made a considerable progress in Comenius's 'Janua,' and had a strong passion for Greek."

Grant that this may be a little abated, because a very serious man is not to be too much believed when he is describing what he admires; it is the very fact of his admiration that is so curious a sign of those hasty times. All being favorable, the child of Evelyn's studious home would have done all these things in the course of nature within a few years. It was the fact that he did them out of the course of nature that was, to Evelyn, so exquisite. The course of nature had not any beauty in his eyes. It might be borne with for the sake of the end, but it was not admired for the majesty of its unhasting process. Jeremy Taylor mourns with him "the strangely hopeful child," who—without Comenius's "Janua" and without congruous syntax—was fulfilling, had they known it, an appropriate hope, answering a distinctive prophecy, and crowning and closing a separate expectation every day of his five years.

Ah! the word "hopeful" seems, to us, in this day, a word too flattering to the estate of man. They thought their little boy strangely hopeful because he was so quick on his way to be something else. They lost the timely perfection the while they were so intent upon their hopes. And yet it is our own modern age that is charged with haste!

It would seem rather as though the world, whatever it shall unlearn, must rightly learn to confess the passing and irrevocable hour; not slighting it, or bidding it hasten its work, nor yet hailing it, with Faust, "Stay, thou art so fair!" Childhood is but change made gay and visible, and the world has lately been converted to change.

Our fathers valued change for the sake of its results; we value it in the act. To us the change is revealed as perpetual; every passage is a goal, and every goal a passage. The hours are equal; but some of them wear apparent wings.

Tout passe. Is the fruit for the flower, or the flower for the fruit, or the fruit for the seeds which it is formed to shelter and contain? It seems as though our forefathers had answered this question most arbitrarily as to the life of man.

All their literature dealing with children is bent upon this haste, this suppression of the approach to what seemed then the only time of fulfilment. The way was without rest to them. And this because they had the illusion of a rest to be gained at some later point of this unpausing life.

Evelyn and his contemporaries dropped the very word child as soon as might be, if not sooner. When a poor little boy came to be eight years old they called him a youth. The diarist himself had no cause to be proud of his own early years, for he was so far indulged in idleness by an "honoured grandmother" that he was "not initiated into any rudiments" till he was four years of age. He seems even to have been a youth of eight before Latin was seriously begun; but this fact he is evidently, in after years, with a total lack of a sense of humour, rather ashamed of, and hardly acknowledges. It is difficult to imagine what childhood must have been when nobody, looking on, saw any fun in it; when everything that was proper to five years old was defect. A strange good conceit of themselves and of their own ages had those fathers.

They took their children seriously, without relief. Evelyn has nothing to say about his little ones that has a sign of a smile in it. Twice are children, not his own, mentioned in his diary. Once he goes to the wedding of a maid of five years old—a curious thing, but not, evidently, an occasion of sensibility. Another time he stands by, in a French hospital, while a youth of less than nine years of age undergoes a frightful surgical operation "with extraordinary patience." "The use I made of it was to give Almighty God hearty thanks that I had not been subject to this deplorable infirmitie." This is what he says.

See, moreover, how the fashion of hurrying childhood prevailed in literature, and how it abolished little girls. It may be that there were in all ages—even those—certain few boys who insisted upon being children; whereas the girls were docile to the adult ideal. Art, for example, had no little girls. There was always Cupid, and there were the prosperous urchin-angels of the painters; the one who is hauling up his little brother by the hand in the "Last Communion of St. Jerome" might be called Tommy. But there were no "little radiant girls." Now and then an "Education of the Virgin" is the exception, and then it is always a matter of sewing and reading. As for the little girl saints, even when they were so young that their hands, like those of St. Agnes, slipped through their fetters, they are always recorded as refusing importunate suitors, which seems necessary to make them interesting to the mediaeval mind, but mars them for ours.

So does the hurrying and ignoring of little-girl-childhood somewhat hamper the delight with which readers of John Evelyn admire his most admirable Mrs. Godolphin. She was Maid of Honour to the Queen in the Court of Charles II. She was, as he prettily says, an Arethusa "who passed through all those turbulent waters without so much as the least stain or tincture in her christall." She held her state with men and maids for her servants, guided herself by most exact rules, such as that of never speaking to the King, gave an excellent example and instruction to the other maids of honour, was "severely careful how she might give the least countenance to that liberty which the gallants there did usually assume," refused the addresses of the "greatest persons," and was as famous for her beauty as for her wit. One would like to forget the age at which she did these things. When she began her service she was eleven. When she was making her rule never to speak to the King she was not thirteen.

Marriage was the business of daughters of fourteen and fifteen, and heroines, therefore, were of those ages. The poets turned April into May, and seemed to think that they lent a grace to the year if they shortened and abridged the spring of their many songs. The particular year they sang of was to be a particularly fine year, as who should say a fine child and forward, with congruous syntax at two years old, and ellipses, figures, and tropes. Even as late as Keats a poet would not have patience with the process of the seasons, but boasted of untimely flowers. The "musk-rose" is never in fact the child of mid-May, as he has it.

The young women of Addison are nearly fourteen years old. His fear of losing the idea of the bloom of their youth makes him so tamper with the bloom of their childhood. The young heiress of seventeen in the *Spectator* has looked upon herself as marriageable "for the last six years." The famous letter describing the figure, the dance, the wit, the stockings of the charming Mr. Shapely is supposed to be written by a girl of thirteen, "willing to settle in the world as soon as she can." She adds, "I have a good portion which they cannot hinder me of." This correspondent is one of "the women who seldom ask advice before they have bought their wedding clothes." There was no sense of childhood in an age that could think this an opportune pleasantry.

But impatience of the way and the wayfaring was to disappear from a later century—an age that has found all things to be on a journey, and all things complete in their day because it is their day, and has its appointed end. It is the tardy conviction of this, rather than a sentiment ready made, that has caused the childhood of children to seem, at last, something else than a defect.

OUT OF TOWN

To be on a *villeggiatura* with the children is to surprise them in ways and words not always evident in the London house. The narrow lodgings cause you to hear and overhear. Nothing is more curious to listen to than a young child's dramatic voice. The child, being a boy, assumes a deep, strong, and ultra-masculine note, and a swagger in his walk, and gives himself the name of the tallest of his father's friends. The tone is not only manly; it is a tone of affairs, and withal careless; it is intended to suggest business, and also the possession of a top-hat and a pipe, and is known in the family of the child as his "official voice." One day it became more official than ever, and really more masculine than life; and it alternated with his own tones of three years old. In these, he asked with humility, "Will you let me go to heaven if I'm naughty? Will you?" Then he gave the reply in the tone of affairs, the official voice at its very best: "No, little boy, I won't!" It was evident that the infant was not assuming the character of his father's tallest friend this time, but had taken a rôle more exalted. His little sister of a year older seemed thoroughly to enjoy the humour of the situation. "Listen to him, mother. He's trying to talk like God. He often does."

Bulls are made by a less imaginative child who likes to find some reason for things—a girl. Out at the work of picking blackberries, she explains, "Those rather good ones were all bad, mother, so I ate them." Being afraid of dogs, this little girl of four years old has all kinds of dodges to disguise her fear, which she has evidently resolved to keep to herself. She will set up a sudden song to distract attention from the fact that she is placing herself out of the dog's way, and she will pretend to turn to gather a flower, while she watches the creature out of sight. On the other hand, prudence in regard to carts and bicycles is openly displayed, and the infants are zealous to warn one another. A rider and his horse are called briefly "a norseback."

Children, who see more things than they have names for, show a fine courage in taking any words that seem likely to serve them, without wasting time in asking for the word in use. This enterprise is most active at three and four years, when children have more than they can say. So a child of those years running to pick up horse-chestnuts, for him a new species, calls after his mother a full description of what he has found, naming the things indifferently "dough-nuts" and "cocoa-nuts." And another, having an anecdote to tell concerning the Thames and a little brook that joins it near the house, calls the first the "front-sea" and the second the "back-sea." There is no intention of taking liberties with the names of things—only a cheerful resolve to go on in spite of obstacles. It is such a spirit of liberty as most of us have felt when we have dreamt of improvising a song or improvising a dance. The child improvises with such means as he has.

This is, of course, at the very early ages. A little later—at eight or nine—there is a very clear-headed sense of the value of words. So that a little girl of that age, told that she may buy some fruit, and wishing to know her limits in spending, asks, "What mustn't it be more than?" For a child, who has not the word "maximum" at hand, nothing could be more precise and concise. Still later, there is a sweet brevity that looks almost like conscious expression, as when a boy writes from his first boarding school: "Whenever I can't stop laughing I have only to think of home."

Infinitely different as children are, they differ in nothing more than in the degree of generosity. The most sensitive of children is a little gay girl whose feelings are hurt with the greatest facility, and who seems, indeed, to have the susceptibilty of other ages as well as of her own—for instance, she cannot endure without a flush of pain to hear herself called fat. But she always brings her little wound to him who has wounded her. The first confidant she seeks is the offender. If you have laughed at her she will not hide her tears elsewhere than on your shoulder. She confesses by her exquisite action at one her poor vanity and her humility.

The worst of children in the country is their inveterate impulse to use death as their toy. Immediately on their discovery of some pretty insect, one tender child calls to the other "Dead it."

Children do not look at the sky unless it is suggested to them to do so. When the sun dips to the narrow horizon of their stature, and comes to the level of their eyes, even then they are not greatly interested. Enormous clouds, erect, with the sun behind, do not gain their eyes. What is of annual interest is the dark. Having fallen asleep all the summer by daylight, and having awakened after sunrise, children find a stimulus of fun and fear in the autumn darkness outside the windows. There is a frolic with the unknown blackness, with the reflections, and with the country night.

EXPRESSION

Strange to say, the eyes of children, whose minds are so small, express intelligence better than do the greater number of adult eyes. David Garrick's were evidently unpreoccupied, like theirs. The look of intelligence is outward—frankly directed upon external things; it is observant, and therefore mobile without inner restlessness. For restless eyes are the least observant of all—they move by a kind of distraction. The looks of observant eyes, moving with the living things they keep in sight, have many pauses as well as flights. This is the action of intelligence, whereas the eyes of intellect are detained or darkened.

Rational perception, with all its phases of humour, are best expressed by a child, who has few second thoughts to divide the image of his momentary feeling. His simplicity adds much to the manifestation of his intelligence. The child is the last and lowest of rational creatures, for in him the "rational soul" closes its long downward flight with the bright final revelation.

He has also the chief beauty of the irrational soul of the mind, that is, of the lower animal—which is singleness. The simplicity, the integrity, the one thing at a time, of a good animal's eyes is a great beauty, and is apt to cause us to exaggerate our sense of their expressiveness. An animal's eyes, at their best, are very slightly expressive; languor or alertness, the quick expectation, even the aloofness of doubt they are able to show, but the showing is mechanical; the human sentiment of the spectator adds the rest.

All this simplicity the child has, at moments, with the divisions and delicacies of the rational soul, also. His looks express the first, the last, and the clearest humanity. He is the first by his youth and the last by his lowliness. He is the beginning and the result of the creation of man.

UNDER THE EARLY STARS

Play is not for every hour of the day, or for any hour taken at random. There is a tide in the affairs of children. Civilization is cruel in sending them to bed at the most stimulating time of dusk. Summer dusk, especially, is the frolic moment for children, baffle them how you may. They may have been in a pottering mood all day, intent upon all kinds of close industries, breathing hard over choppings and poundings. But when late twilight comes, there comes also the punctual wildness. The children will run and pursue, and laugh for the mere movement—it does so jog their spirits.

What remembrances does this imply of the hunt, what of the predatory dark? The kitten grows alert at the same hour, and hunts for moths and crickets in the grass. It comes like an imp, leaping on all fours. The children lie in ambush and fall upon one another in the mimicry of hunting.

The sudden outbreak of action is complained of as a defiance and a rebellion. Their entertainers are tired, and the children are to go home. But, with more or less of life and fire, they strike some blow for liberty. It may be the impotent revolt of the ineffectual child, or the stroke of the conqueror; but something, something is done for freedom under the early stars.

This is not the only time when the energy of children is in conflict with the weariness of men. But it is less tolerable that the energy of men should be at odds with the weariness of children, which happens at some time of their jaunts together, especially, alas! in the jaunts of the poor.

Of games for the summer dusk when it rains, cards are most beloved by children. Three tiny girls were to be taught "old maid" to beguile the time. One of them, a nut-brown child of five, was persuading another to play. "Oh come," she said, "and play with me at new maid."

The time of falling asleep is a child's immemorial and incalculable hour. It is full of traditions, and beset by antique habits. The habit of prehistoric races has been cited as the only explanation of the fixity of some customs in mankind. But if the enquirers who appeal to that beginning remembered better their own infancy, they would seek no further. See the habits in falling to sleep which have children in their thralldom. Try to overcome them in any child, and his own conviction of their high antiquity weakens your hand.

Childhood is antiquity, and with the sense of time and the sense of mystery is connected for ever the hearing of a lullaby. The French sleep-song is the most romantic. There is in it such a sound of history as must inspire any imaginative child, falling to sleep, with a sense of the incalculable; and the songs themselves are old. *Le Bon Roi Dagobert* has been sung over French cradles since the legend was fresh. The nurse knows nothing more sleepy than the tune and the verse that she herself slept to when a child. The gaiety of the thirteenth century, in *Le Pont a' Avignon*, is put mysteriously to sleep, away in the *tête à tête of* child and nurse, in a thousand little sequestered rooms at night. *Malbrook* would be comparatively modern, were not all things that are sung to a drowsing child as distant as the day of Abraham.

If English children are not rocked to many such aged lullabies, some of them are put to sleep to strange cradle-songs. The affectionate races that are brought into subjection sing the primitive lullaby to the white child. Asiatic voices and African persuade him to sleep in the tropical night. His closing eyes are filled with alien images.

THE MAN WITH TWO HEADS

It is generally understood in the family that the nurse who menaces a child, whether with the supernatural or with simple sweeps, lions, or tigers—goes. The rule is a right one, for the appeal to fear may possibly hurt a child; nevertheless, it oftener fails to hurt him. If he is prone to fears, he will be helpless under their grasp, without the help of human tales. The night will threaten him, the shadow will pursue, the dream will catch him; terror itself have him by the heart. And terror, having made his pulses leap, knows how to use any thought, any shape, any image, to account to the child's mind for the flight and tempest of his blood. "The child shall not be frightened," decrees ineffectual love; but though no man make him afraid, he is frightened. Fear knows him well and finds him alone.

Such a child is hardly at the mercy of any human rashness and impatience; nor is the child whose pulses go steadily, and whose brows are fresh and cool, at their mercy. This is one of the points upon which a healthy child resembles the Japanese. Whatever that extreme Oriental may be in war and diplomacy, whatever he may be at London University, or whatever his plans of Empire, in relation to the unseen world he is a child at play. He hides himself, he hides his eyes and pretends to believe that he is hiding, he runs from the supernatural and laughs for the fun of running.

So did a child, threatened for his unruliness with the revelation of the man with two heads. The nurse must have had recourse to this man under acute provocation. The boy, who had profited well by every one of his four long years, and was radiant with the light and colour of health, refused to be left to compose himself to sleep. That act is an adult act, learnt in the self-conscious and deliberate years of later life, when man goes on a mental journey in search of rest, aware of setting forth. But the child is pursued and overtaken by sleep, caught, surprised, and overcome. He goes no more to sleep, than he takes a "constitutional" with his hoop and hoopstick. The child amuses himself up to the last of his waking moments. Happily, in the search for amusement, he is apt to learn some habit or to cherish some toy, either of which may betray him and deliver him up to sleep, the enemy. What wonder, then, if a child who knows that everyone in the world desires his peace and pleasure, should clamour for companionship in the first reluctant minutes of bed? This child, being happy, did not weep for what he wanted; he shouted for it in the rousing tones of his strength. After many evenings of this he was told that this was precisely the vociferous kind of wakefulness that might cause the man with two heads to show himself.

Unable to explain that no child ever goes to sleep, but that sleep, on the contrary, "goes" for a child, the little boy yet accepted the penalty, believed in the man, and kept quiet for a time.

There was indignation in the mother's heart when the child instructed her as to what might be looked for at his bedside; she used all her emphasis in assuring him that no man with two heads would ever trouble those innocent eyes, for there was no such portent anywhere on earth. There is no such heart-oppressing task as the making of these assurances to a child, for whom who knows what portents are actually in wait! She found him, however, cowering with laughter, not with dread, lest the man with two heads should see or overhear. The man with two heads had become his play, and so was perhaps bringing about his sleep by gentler means than the nurse had intended. The man was employing the vacant minutes of the little creature's flight from sleep, called "going to sleep" in the inexact language of the old.

Nor would the boy give up his faith with its tremor and private laughter. Because a child has a place for everything, this boy had placed the monstrous man in the ceiling, in a corner of the room that might be kept out of sight by the bed curtain. If that corner were left uncovered, the fear would grow stronger than the fun; "the man would see me," said the little boy. But let the curtain be in position, and the child lay alone, hugging the dear belief that the monster was near.

He was earnest in controversy with his mother as to the existence of his man. The man was there, for he had been told so, and he was there to wait for "naughty boys," said the child, with cheerful self-condemnation. The little boy's voice was somewhat hushed, because of the four ears of the listener, but it did not falter, except when his mother's arguments against the existence of the man seemed to him cogent and likely to gain the day. Then for the first time the boy was a little downcast, and the light of mystery became dimmer in his gay eyes.

CHILDREN IN BURLESQUE

Derision, which is so great a part of human comedy, has not spared the humours of children. Yet they are fitter subjects for any other kind of jesting. In the first place they are quite defenceless, but besides and before this, it might have been supposed that nothing in a child could provoke the equal passion of scorn. Between confessed unequals scorn is not even suggested. Its derisive proclamation of inequality has no sting and no meaning where inequality is natural and manifest.

Children rouse the laughter of men and women; but in all that laughter the tone of derision is more strange a discord than the tone of anger would be, or the tone of theological anger and menace. These, little children have had to bear in their day, but in the grim and serious moods—not in the play—of their elders. The wonder is that children should ever have been burlesqued, or held to be fit subjects for irony.

Whether the thing has been done anywhere out of England, in any form, might be a point for enquiry. It would seem, at a glance, that English art and literature are quite alone in this incredible manner of sport.

And even here, too, the thing that is laughed at in a child is probably always a mere reflection of the parents' vulgarity. None the less it is an unintelligible thing that even the rankest vulgarity of father or mother should be resented, in the child, with the implacable resentment of derision.

John Leech used the caricature of a baby for the purposes of a scorn that was not angry, but familiar. It is true that the poor child had first been burlesqued by the unchildish aspect imposed upon him by his dress, which presented him, without the beauties of art or nature, to all the unnatural ironies. Leech did but finish him in the same spirit, with dots for the childish eyes, and a certain form of face which is best described as a fat square containing two circles—the inordinate cheeks of that ignominious baby. That is the child as *Punch* in Leech's day preserved him, the latest figure of the then prevailing domestic raillery of the domestic.

In like manner did Thackeray and Dickens, despite all their sentiment. Children were made to serve both the sentiment and the irony between which those two writers, alike in this, stood double-minded. Thackeray, writing of his snobs, wreaks himself upon a child; there is no worse snob than his snob-child. There are snob-children not only in the book dedicated to their parents, but in nearly all his novels. There is a female snob-child in "Lovel the Widower," who may be taken as a type, and there are snob-children at frequent intervals in "Philip." It is not certain that Thackeray intended the children of Pendennis himself to be innocent and exempt.

In one of Dickens's early sketches there is a plot amongst the humorous *dramatis personae*, to avenge themselves on a little boy for the lack of tact whereby his parents have brought him with them to a party on the river. The principal humorist frightens the child into convulsions. The incident is the success of the day, and is obviously intended to have some kind of reflex action in amusing the reader. In Dickens's maturer books the burlesque little girl imitates her mother's illusory fainting-fits.

Our glimpses of children in the fugitive pages of that day are grotesque. A little girl in *Punch* improves on the talk of her dowdy mother with the maids. An inordinate baby stares; a little boy flies, hideous, from some hideous terror.

AUTHORSHIP

Authorship prevails in nurseries—at least in some nurseries. In many it is probably a fitful game, and since the days of the Brontës there has not been a large family without its magazine. The weak point of all this literature is its commonplace. The child's effort is to write something as much like as possible to the tedious books that are read to him; he is apt to be fluent and foolish. If a child simple enough to imitate were also simple enough not to imitate he might write nursery magazines that would not bore us.

As it is, there is sometimes nothing but the fresh and courageous spelling to make his stories go. "He," however, is hardly the pronoun. The girls are the more active authors, and the more prosaic. What they would write had they never read things written for them by the dull, it is not possible to know. What they do write is this—to take a passage: "Poor Mrs. Bald (that was her name) thought she would never get to the wood where her aunt lived, she got down and pulled the donky on by the bridal . . . Alas! her troubles were not over yet, the donky would not go where she wanted it, instead of turning down Rose Lane it went down another, which although Mrs. Bald did not know it led to a very deep and dangerous pond. The donky ran into the pond and Mrs. Bald was dround."

To give a prosperous look to the magazine containing the serial story just quoted, a few pages of mixed advertisements are laboriously written out: "The Imatation of Christ is the best book in all the world." "Read Thompson's poetry and you are in a world of delight." "Barrat's ginger beer is the only ginger beer to drink." "The place for a ice." Under the indefinite heading "A Article," readers are told "that they are liable to read the paper for nothing."

A still younger hand contributes a short story in which the hero returns to his home after a report of his death had been believed by his wife and family. The last sentence is worth quoting: "We will now," says the author, "leave Mrs. White and her two children to enjoy the sudden appearance of Mr. White."

Here is an editorial announcement: "Ladies and gentlemen, every week at the end of the paper there will be a little article on the habits of the paper."

On the whole, authorship does not seem to foster the quality of imagination. Convention, during certain early years, may be a very strong motive—not so much with children brought up strictly within its limits, perhaps, as with those who have had an exceptional freedom. Against this, as a kind of childish bohemianism, there is, in one phase of childhood, a strong reaction. To one child, brought up internationally, and with somewhat too much liberty amongst peasant play-mates and their games, in many dialects, eagerness to become like "other people," and even like the other people of quite inferior fiction, grew to be almost a passion. The desire was in time out-grown, but it cost the girl some years of her simplicity. The style is not always the child.

LETTERS

The letter exacted from a child is usually a letter of thanks; somebody has sent him a box of chocolates. The thanks tend to stiffen a child's style; but in any case a letter is the occasion of a sudden self-consciousness, newer to a child than his elders know. They speak prose and know it. But a young child possesses his words by a different tenure; he is not aware of the spelt and written aspect of the things he says every day; he does not dwell upon the sound of them. He is so little taken by the kind and character of any word that he catches the first that comes at random. A little child to whom a peach was first revealed, whispered to his mother, "I like that kind of turnip." Compelled to write a letter, the child finds the word of daily life suddenly a stranger.

The fresher the mind the duller the sentence; and the younger the fingers the older, more wrinkled, and more sidling the handwriting. Dickens, who used his eyes, remarked the contrast. The hand of a child and his face are full of rounds; but his written O is tottering and haggard.

His phrases are ceremonious without the dignity of ceremony. The child chatters because he wants his companion to hear; but there is no inspiration in the act of writing to a distant aunt about whom he probably has some grotesque impression because he cannot think of anyone, however vague and forgotten, without a mental image. As like as not he pictures all his relatives at a distance with their eyes shut. No boy wants to write familiar things to a forgotten aunt with her eyes shut. His thoughtless elders require him not only to write to her under these discouragements, but to write to her in an artless and childlike fashion.

The child is unwieldy of thought, besides. He cannot send the conventional messages but he loses his way among the few pronouns: "I send them their love," "They sent me my love," "I kissed their hand to me." If he is stopped and told to get the words right, he has to make a long effort. His precedent might be cited to excuse every politician who cannot remember whether he began his sentence with "people" in the singular or the plural, and who finishes it otherwise than as he began it. Points of grammar that are purely points of logic baffle a child completely. He is as unready in the thought needed for these as he is in the use of his senses.

It is not true—though it is generally said—that a young child's senses are quick. This is one of the unverified ideas that commend themselves, one knows not why. We have had experiments to compare the relative quickness of perception proved by men and women. The same experiments with children would give curious results, but they can hardly, perhaps, be made, because the children would be not only slow to perceive but slow to announce the perception; so the moment would go by, and the game be lost. Not even amateur conjuring does so baffle the slow turning of a child's mind as does a little intricacy of grammar.

THE FIELDS

The pride of rustic life is the child's form of caste-feeling. The country child is the aristocrat; he has *des relations suivies* with game-keepers, nay, with the most interesting mole-catchers. He has a perfectly self-conscious joy that he is not in a square or a suburb. No essayist has so much feeling against terraces and villas.

As for imitation country—the further suburb—it is worse than town; it is a place to walk in; and the tedium of a walk to a child's mind is hardly measurable by a man, who walks voluntarily, with his affairs to think about, and his eyes released, by age, from the custom of perpetual observation. The child, compelled to walk, is the only unresting observer of the asphalt, the pavement, the garden gates and railings, and the tedious people. He is bored as he will never be bored when a man.

He is at his best where, under the welcome stress and pressure of abundant crops, he is admitted to the labours of men and women, neither in mere play nor in the earnest of the hop-field for the sake of his little gains. On the steep farm lands of the Canton de Vaud, where maize and grapes are carried in the *botte*, so usually are children expected in the field that *bottes* are made to the shape of a back and arms of five years old. Some, made for harvesters of those years, can hold no more than a single yellow ear of maize or two handfuls of beans. You may meet the same little boy with the repetitions of this load a score of times in the morning. Moreover the Swiss mother has always a fit sense of what is due to that labourer. When the plums are gathered, for instance, she bakes in the general village oven certain round open tarts across which her arm can hardly reach. No plum tarts elsewhere are anything but dull in comparison with these. There is, besides, the first loaf from the new flour, brown from the maize and white from the wheat. Nor can a day of potato-gathering be more appropriately ended than with a little fire built afield and the baking of some of the harvest under the wood ashes. Vintaging needs no praises, nor does apple-gathering; even when the apples are for cider, they are never acrid enough to baffle a child's tooth.

Yet even those children who are so unlucky as never to have worked in a real field, but have been compelled to vary their education with nothing but play, are able to comfort themselves with the irregular harvest of the hedges. They have no little hand in the realities of cultivation, but wild growths give them blackberries. Pale are the joys of nutting beside those of haymaking, but at least they are something.

Harvests apart, Spring, not Autumn, should make a childhood of memories for the future. In later Autumn, life is speeding away, ebbing, taking flight, a fugitive, taking disguises, hiding in the dry seed, retreating into the dark. The daily progress of things in Spring is for children, who look close. They know the way of moss and the roots of ivy, they breathe the breath of earth immediately, direct. They have a sense of place, of persons, and of the past that may be remembered but cannot be recaptured. Adult accustomed eyes cannot see what a child's eye sees of the personality of a person; to the child the accidents of voice and look are charged with separate and unique character. Such a sense of place as he got in a day within some forest, or in a week by some lake, so that a sound or odour can bring it back in after days, with a shock—even such a sense of single personality does a little watchful girl get from the accents, the turns of the head, the habits of the hands, the presence of a woman. Not all places, nor all persons, are so quick with the expression of themselves; the child knows the difference. As for places that are so loaded, and that breathe so, the child discerns them passionately.

A travelled child multiplies these memories and has them in their variety. His heart has room for many places that have the spirit of place. The glacier may be forgotten, but some little tract of pasture that has taken wing to the head of a mountain valley, a field that has soared up a pass unnamed, will become a memory, in time, sixty years old. That is a fortunate child who has tasted country life in places far apart, who has helped, followed the wheat to the threshing-floor of a Swiss village, stumbled after a plough of Virgil's shape in remoter Tuscan hills, and gleaned after a vintage. You cannot suggest pleasanter memories than those of the vintage, for the day when the wine will be old.

THE BARREN SHORE

It may be a disappointment to the children each year at play upon so many beaches—even if they are but dimly aware of their lack—to find their annual plaything to be not a real annual; an annual thing, indeed, to them, for the arbitrary reason that they go down to it once a year, but not annual in the vital and natural sense of the seasons, not waxing and waning, not bearing, not turning that circle of the seasons whereof no one knows which is the highest point and the secret and the ultimate purpose, not recreated, not new, and not yielding to the child anything raw and irregular to eat.

Sand castles are well enough, and they are the very commonplace of the recollections of elders, of their rhetoric, and of what they think appropriate for their young ones. Shingle and sand are good playthings, but absolute play is not necessarily the ideal of a child; he would rather have a frolic of work. Of all the early autumn things to be done in holiday time, that game with the beach and the wave is the least good for holiday-time.

Not that the shore is everywhere so barren. The coast of the Londoners— all round the southern and eastern borders of England—is indeed the dullest of all sea-margins. But away in the gentle bays of Jersey the summer grows a crop of seaweed which the long ocean wave leaves in noble curves upon the beach; for under sunny water the storms have gathered the crops. The Channel Island people go gleaning after the sea, and store the seaweed for their fields. Thus the beaches of Jersey bays are not altogether barren, and have a kind of dead and accessory harvest for the farmer. After a night of storm these crops are stacked and carted and carried, the sea-wind catching away loose shreds from the summits of the loads.

Further south, if the growth of the sea is not so put to use, the shore has yet its seasons. You could hardly tell, if you did not know the month, whether a space of sea or a series of waves, at Aldborough, say, or at Dover, were summer or winter water; but in those fortunate regions which are southern, yet not too southern for winter, and have thus the strongest swing of change and the fullest pulse of the year, there are a winter sea and a summer sea, brilliantly different, with a delicate variety between the hastening blue of spring and the lingering blue of September. There you bathe from the rocks, untroubled by tides, and unhurried by chills, and with no incongruous sun beating on your head while your fingers are cold. You bathe when the sun has set, and the vast sea has not a whisper; you know a rock in the distance where you can rest; and where you float, there float also by you opalescent jelly-fish, half transparent in the perfectly transparent water. An hour in the warm sea is not enough. Rock-bathing is done on lonely shores. A city may be but a mile away, and the cultivated vineyards may be close above the seaside pine-trees, but the place is perfectly remote. You pitch your tent on any little hollow of beach. A charming Englishwoman who used to bathe with her children under the great rocks of her Mediterranean villa in the motionless white evenings of summer put white roses in her hair, and liked to sit out on a rock at sea where the first rays of the moon would touch her.

You bathe in the Channel in the very prose of the day. Nothing in the world is more uninteresting than eleven o'clock. It is the hour of mediocrity under the best conditions; but eleven o'clock on a shingly beach, in a half-hearted summer, is a very common thing. Twelve has a dignity always, and everywhere its name is great. The noon of every day that ever dawned is in its place heroic; but eleven is worldly. One o'clock has an honest human interest to the hungry child, and every hour of the summer afternoon, after three, has the grace of deepening and lingering life. To bathe at eleven in the sun, in the wind, to bathe from a machine, in a narrow sea that is certainly not clear and is only by courtesy clean, to bathe in obedience to a tyrannical tide and in water that is always much colder than yourself, to bathe in a hurry and in public—this is to know nothing rightly of one of the greatest of all the pleasures that humanity takes with nature.

By the way, the sea of Jersey has more the character of a real sea than of mere straits. These temperate islands would be better called the Ocean Islands. When Edouard Pailleron was a boy and wrote poetry, he composed a letter to Victor Hugo, the address whereof was a matter of some thought. The final decision was to direct it, "A Victor Hugo, Océan." It reached him. It even received a reply: "I am the Past, you are the Future; I am, etc." If an English boy had had the same idea the name of the Channel Islands would have spoilt it. "A Victor Hugo, La Manche," would hardly have interested the postal authorities so much; but "the Channel" would have had no respect at all. Indeed, this last is suggestive of nothing but steamers and of grey skies inland—formless grey skies, undesigned, with their thin cloud torn to slender rags by a perpetual wind.

As for the children, to whom belongs the margin of the sea, machine-bathing at eleven o'clock will hardly furnish them with a magical early memory. Time was when this was made penitential to them, like the rest of life, upon a principle that no longer prevails. It was vulgarized for them and made violent. A bathing woman, type of all ugliness in their sensitive eyes, came striding, shapeless, through the unfriendly sea, seized them if they were very young, ducked them, and returned them to the chilly machine, generally in the futile and superfluous saltness of tears. "Too much of water had they," poor infants.

None the less is the barren shore the children's; and St. Augustine, Isaac Newton, and Wordsworth had not a vision of sea-beaches without a child there.

THE BOY

After an infancy of more than common docility and a young childhood of few explicit revolts, the boy of twelve years old enters upon a phase which the bystander may not well understand but may make shift to note as an impression.

Like other subtle things, his position is hardly to be described but by negatives. Above all, he is not demonstrative. The days are long gone by when he said he wanted a bicycle, a top hat, and a pipe. One or two of these things he has, and he takes them without the least swagger. He avoids expression of any kind. Any satisfaction he may feel with things as they are is rather to be surprised in his manner than perceived in his action. Mr. Jaggers, when it befell him to be astonished, showed it by a stop of manner, for an indivisible moment—not by a pause in the thing he chanced to be about. In like manner the boy cannot prevent his most innocent pleasures from arresting him.

He will not endure (albeit he does not confess so much) to be told to do anything, at least in that citadel of his freedom, his home. His elders probably give him as few orders as possible. He will almost ingeniously evade any that are inevitably or thoughtlessly inflicted upon him, but if he does but succeed in only postponing his obedience, he has, visibly, done something for his own relief. It is less convenient that he should hold mere questions, addressed to him in all good faith, as in some sort an attempt upon his liberty.

Questions about himself one might understand to be an outrage. But it is against impersonal and indifferent questions also that the boy sets his face like a rock. He has no ambition to give information on any point. Older people may not dislike the opportunity, and there are even those who bring to pass questions of a trivial kind for the pleasure of answering them with animation. This, the boy perhaps thinks, is "fuss," and, if he has any passions, he has a passionate dislike of fuss.

When a younger child tears the boy's scrapbook (which is conjectured, though not known, to be the dearest thing he has) he betrays no emotion; that was to be expected. But when the stolen pages are rescued and put by for him, he abstains from taking an interest in the retrieval; he will do nothing to restore them. To do so would mar the integrity of his reserve. If he would do much rather than answer questions, he would suffer something rather than ask them.

He loves his father and a friend of his father's, and he pushes them, in order to show it without compromising his temperament.

He is a partisan in silence. It may be guessed that he is often occupied in comparing other people with his admired men. Of this too he says little, except some brief word of allusion to what other men do *not* do.

When he speaks it is with a carefully shortened vocabulary. As an author shuns monotony, so does the boy shun change. He does not generally talk slang; his habitual words are the most usual of daily words made useful and appropriate by certain varieties of voice. These express for him all that he will consent to communicate. He reserves more by speaking dull words with zeal than by using zealous words that might betray him. But his brevity is the chief thing; he has almost made an art of it.

He is not "merry." Merry boys have pretty manners, and it must be owned that this boy's manners are not pretty. But if not merry, he is happy; there never was a more untroubled soul. If he has an almost grotesque reticence, he has no secrets. Nothing that he thinks is very much hidden. Even if he did not push his father, it would be evident that the boy loves him; even if he never laid his hand (and this little thing he does rarely) on his friend's shoulder, it would be plain that he loves his friend. His happiness appears in his moody and charming face, his ambition in his dumbness, and the hopes of his life to come in ungainly bearing. How does so much heart, how does so much sweetness, all unexpressed, appear? For it is not only those who know him well that know the child's heart; strangers are aware of it. This, which he would not reveal, is the only thing that is quite unmistakable and quite conspicuous.

What he thinks that he turns visibly to the world is a sense of humour, with a measure of criticism and of indifference. What he thinks the world may divine in him is courage and an intelligence. But carry himself how he will, he is manifestly a tender, gentle, and even spiritual creature, masculine and innocent—"a nice boy." There is no other way of describing him than that of his own brief language.

ILLNESS

The patience of young children in illness is a commonplace of some little books, but none the less a fresh fact. In spite of the sentimental, children in illness remain the full sources of perpetual surprises. Their self-control in real suffering is a wonder. A little turbulent girl, brilliant and wild, and unaccustomed, it might be thought, to deal in any way with her own impulses—a child whose way was to cry out, laugh, complain, and triumph without bating anything of her own temperament, and without the hesitation of a moment, struck her face, on a run, against a wall and was cut and in a moment overwhelmed with pain and covered with blood. "Tell mother it's nothing! Tell mother, quick, it's nothing!" cried the magnanimous child as soon as she could speak.

The same child fell over the rail of a staircase and was obliged to lie for some ten days on her back, so that the strained but not broken little body might recover itself. Every movement was, in a measure, painful; and there was a long captivity, a helplessness enforced and guarded by twinges, a constant impossibility to yield to the one thing that had carried her through all her years—impulse. A condition of acute consciousness was imposed upon a creature whose first condition of life had been unconsciousness; and this during the long period of ten of a child's days and nights at eight years old.

Yet during every hour of the time the child was not only gay but patient, not fitfully, but steadily, resigned, sparing of requests, reluctant to be served, inventive of tender and pious little words that she had never used before. "You are exquisite to me, mother," she said, at receiving some common service.

Even in the altering and harassing conditions of fever, a generous child assumes the almost incredible attitude of deliberate patience. Not that illness is to be trusted to work so. There is another child who in his brief indispositions becomes invincible, armed against medicine finally. The last appeal to force, as his distracted elders find, is all but an impossibility;

but in any case it would be a failure. You can bring the spoon to the child, but three nurses cannot make him drink. This, then, is the occasion of the ultimate resistance. He raises the standard of revolution, and casts every tradition and every precept to the wind on which it flies. He has his elders at a disadvantage; for if they pursue him with a grotesque spoon their maxims and commands are, at the moment, still more grotesque. He is committed to the wild novelty of absolute refusal. He not only refuses, moreover, he disbelieves; he throws everything over. Told that the medicine is not so bad, this nihilist laughs.

Medicine apart, a minor ailment is an interest and a joy. "Am I unwell to-day, mother?" asks a child with all his faith and confidence at the highest point.

THE YOUNG CHILD

The infant of literature "wails" and wails feebly, with the invariability of a thing unproved and taken for granted. Nothing, nevertheless, could be more unlike a wail than the most distinctive cry whereon the child of man catches his first breath. It is a hasty, huddled outcry, sharp and brief, rather deep than shrill in tone. With all deference to old moralities, man does not weep at beginning this world; he simply lifts up his new voice much as do the birds in the Zoological Gardens, and with much the same tone as some of the duck kind there. He does not weep for some months to come. His outcry soon becomes the human cry that is better known than loved, but tears belong to later infancy. And if the infant of days neither wails nor weeps, the infant of months is still too young to be gay. A child's mirth, when at last it begins, is his first secret; you understand little of it. The first smile (for the convulsive movement in sleep that is popularly adorned by that name is not a smile) is an uncertain sketch of a smile, unpractised but unmistakable. It is accompanied by a single sound—a sound that would be a monosyllable if it were articulate—which is the utterance, though hardly the communication, of a private jollity. That and that alone is the real beginning of human laughter.

From the end of the first fortnight in life, when it appears for the first time, and as it were flickeringly, the child's smile begins to grow definite and, gradually, more frequent. By very slow degrees the secrecy passes away, and the dryness becomes more genial. The child now smiles more openly, but he is still very unlike the laughing creature of so much prose and verse. His laughter takes a long time to form. The monosyllable grows louder, and then comes to be repeated with little catches of the breath. The humour upon which he learns to laugh is that of something which approaches him quickly and then withdraws. This is the first intelligible jest of jesting man.

An infant never meets your eyes; he evidently does not remark the features of faces near him. Whether because of the greater conspicuousness of dark hair or dark hat, or for some like reason, he addresses his looks, his laughs, and apparently his criticism, to the heads, not the faces, of his friends. These are the ways of all infants, various in character, parentage, race, and colour; they do the same things. There are turns in a kitten's play—arched leapings and sidelong jumps, graceful rearings and grotesque dances—which the sacred kittens of Egypt used in their time. But not more alike are these repetitions than the impulses of all young children learning to laugh.

In regard to the child of a somewhat later growth, we are told much of his effect upon the world; not much of the effect of the world upon him. Yet he is compelled to endure the reflex results, at least, of all that pleases, distresses, or oppresses the world. That he should be obliged to suffer the moods of men is a more important thing than that men should be amused by his moods. If he is saddened, that is certainly much more than that his elders should be gladdened. It is doubtless hardly possible that children should go altogether free of human affairs. They might, in mere justice, be spared the burden they bear ignorantly and simply when it is laid upon them, of such events and ill fortunes as may trouble our peace; but they cannot easily be spared the hearing of a disturbed voice or the sight of an altered face. Alas! they are made to feel money-matters, and even this is not the worst. There are unconfessed worldliness, piques, and rivalries, of which they do not know the names, but which change the faces where they look for smiles. To such alterations children are sensitive even when they seem least accessible to the commands, the warnings, the threats, or the counsels of elders. Of all these they may be gaily independent, and yet may droop when their defied tyrants are dejected.

For though the natural spirit of children is happy, the happiness is a mere impulse and is easily disconcerted. They are gay without knowing any very sufficient reason for being so, and when sadness is, as it were, proposed to them, things fall away from under their feet, they are helpless and find no stay. For this reason the merriest of all children are those, much pitied, who are brought up neither in a family nor in a public home by paid guardians, but in a place of charity, rightly named, where impartial, unalterable, and impersonal devotion has them in hand. They endure an immeasurable loss, and are orphans, but they gain in perpetual gaiety; they live in an unchanging temperature. The separate nest is nature's, and the best; but it might be wished that the separate nest were less subject to moods. The nurse has her private business, and when it does not prosper, and when the remote affairs of the governess go wrong, the child receives the ultimate vibration of the mishap.

The uniformity of infancy passes away long before the age when children have this indefinite suffering inflicted upon them; and they have become infinitely various, and feel the consequences of the cares of their elders in unnumbered degrees. The most charming children feel them the most sensibly, and not with resentment but with sympathy. It is assuredly in the absence of resentment that consists the virtue of childhood. What other thing are we to learn of them? Not simplicity, for they are intricate enough. Not gratitude; for their usual sincere thanklessness makes half the pleasure of doing them good. Not obedience; for the child is born with the love of liberty. And as for humility, the boast of a child is the frankest thing in the world. A child's natural vanity is not merely the delight in his own possessions, but the triumph over others less fortunate. If this emotion were not so young it would be exceedingly unamiable. But the truth must be confessed that having very quickly learnt the value of comparison and relation, a child rejoices in the perception that what he has is better than what his brother has; this comparison is a means of judging his fortune, after all. It is true that if his brother showed distress, he might make haste to offer an exchange. But the impulse of joy is candidly egotistic.

It is the sweet and entire forgiveness of children, who ask pity for their sorrows from those who have caused them, who do not perceive that they are wronged, who never dream that they are forgiving, and who make no bargain for apologies—it is this that men and women are urged to learn of a child. Graces more confessedly childlike they make shift to teach themselves.

FAIR AND BROWN

George Eliot, in one of her novels, has a good-natured mother, who confesses that when she administers justice she is obliged to spare the offenders who have fair hair, because they look so much more innocent than the rest. And if this is the state of maternal feelings where all are more or less fair, what must be the miscarriage of justice in countries where a *blond* angel makes his infrequent visit within the family circle?

In England he is the rule, and supreme as a matter of course. He is "English," and best, as is the early asparagus and the young potato, according to the happy conviction of the shops. To say "child" in England is to say "fair-haired child," even as in Tuscany to say "young man" is to say "tenor." "I have a little party to-night, eight or ten tenors, from neighbouring palazzi, to meet my English friends."

But France is a greater enthusiast than our now country. The fairness and the golden hair are here so much a matter of orthodoxy, that they are not always mentioned; they are frequently taken for granted. Not so in France; the French go out of their way to make the exceptional fairness of their children the rule of their literature. No French child dare show his face in a book—prose or poetry—without blue eyes and fair hair. It is a thing about which the French child of real life can hardly escape a certain sensitiveness. What, he may ask, is the use of being a dark-haired child of fact, when all the emotion, all the innocence, all the romance, are absorbed by the flaxen-haired child of fiction? How deplorable that our mothers, the French infants may say, should have their unattained ideals in the nurseries of the imagination; how dismal that they should be perpetually disillusioned in the nurseries of fact! Is there then no sentiment for us? they may ask. Will not convention, which has been forced to restore the advantage to truth on so many other points, be compelled to yield on this point also, and reconcile our aunts to the family colouring?

All the schools of literature are in a tale. The classic masters, needless to say, do not stoop to the colouring of boys and girls; but as soon as the

Romantiques arise, the cradle is there, and no soft hair ever in it that is not of some tone of gold, no eyes that are not blue, and no cheek that is not white and pink as milk and roses. Victor Hugo, who discovered the child of modern poetry, never omits the touch of description; the word *blond* is as inevitable as any epithet marshalled to attend its noun in a last-century poet's dictionary. One would not have it away; one can hear the caress with which the master pronounces it, "making his mouth," as Swift did for his "little language." Nor does the customary adjective fail in later literature. It was dear to the Realist, and it is dear to the Symbolist. The only difference is that in the French of the Symbolist it precedes the noun.

And yet it is time that the sweetness of the dark child should have its day. He is really no less childlike than the other. There is a pretty antithesis between the strong effect of his colouring and the softness of his years and of his months. The blond human being—man, woman or child—has the beauty of harmony; the hair plays off from the tones of the flesh, only a few degrees brighter or a few degrees darker. Contrast of colour there is, in the blue of the eyes, and in the red of cheek and lip, but there is no contrast of tone. The whole effect is that of much various colour and of equal tone. In the dark face there is hardly any colour and an almost complete opposition of tone. The complete opposition, of course, would be black and white; and a beautiful dark child comes near to this, but for the lovely modifications, the warmth of his white, and of his black alike, so that the one tone, as well as the other, is softened towards brown. It is the beauty of contrast, with a suggestion of harmony—as it were a beginning of harmony—which is infinitely lovely.

Nor is the dark child lacking in variety. His radiant eyes range from a brown so bright that it looks golden in the light, to a brown so dark that it barely defines the pupil. So is his hair various, answering the sun with unsuspected touches, not of gold but of bronze. And his cheek is not invariably pale. A dusky rose sometimes lurks there with such an effect of vitality as you will hardly get from the shallower pink of the flaxened haired. And the suggestion is that of late summer, the colour of wheat almost ready for the harvest, and darker, redder flowers—poppies and others—than come in Spring.

The dark eyes, besides, are generally brighter—they shelter a more liquid light than the blue or grey. Southern eyes have generally most beautiful whites. And as to the charm of the childish figure, there is usually an infantine slenderness in the little Southener that is at least as young and sweet as the round form of the blond child. And yet the painters of Italy would have none of it. They rejected the dusky brilliant pale little Italians all about them; they would have none but flaxen-haired children, and they would have nothing that was slim, nothing that was thin, nothing that was shadowy. They rejoiced in much fair flesh, and in all possible freshness. So it was in fair Flanders as well as in dark Italy. But so it was not in Spain. The Pyrenees seemed to interrupt the tradition. And as Murillo saw the charm of dark heads, and the innocence of dark eyes, so did one English painter. Reynolds painted young dark hair as tenderly as the youngest gold.

REAL CHILDHOOD

The world is old because its history is made up of successive childhoods and of their impressions. Your hours when you were six were the enormous hours of the mind that has little experience and constant and quick forgetfulness. Therefore when your mother's visitor held you so long at his knee, while he talked to her the excited gibberish of the grown-up, he little thought what he forced upon you; what the things he called minutes really were, measured by a mind unused; what passive and then what desperate weariness he held you to by his slightly gesticulating hands that pressed some absent-minded caress, rated by you at its right value, in the pauses of his anecdotes. You, meanwhile, were infinitely tired of watching the play of his conversing moustache.

Indeed, the contrast of the length of contemporary time (this pleonasm is inevitable) is no small mystery, and the world has never had the wit fully to confess it.

You remembered poignantly the special and singular duration of some such space as your elders, perhaps, called half-an-hour—so poignantly that you spoke of it to your sister, not exactly with emotion, but still as a dreadful fact of life. You had better instinct than to complain of it to the talkative, easy-living, occupied people, who had the management of the world in their hands—your seniors. You remembered the duration of some such separate half-hour so well that you have in fact remembered it until now, and so now, of course, will never forget it.

As to the length of Beethoven, experienced by you on duty in the drawing room, it would be curious to know whether it was really something greater than Beethoven had any idea of. You sat and listened, and tried to fix a passage in your mind as a kind of half-way mark, with the deliberate provident intention of helping yourself through the time during a future hearing; for you knew too well that you would have to bear it all again. You could not do the same with sermons, because, though even more fatiguing, they were more or less different each time.

While your elders passed over some particularly tedious piece of road—and a very tedious piece of road existed within short distance of every house you lived in or stayed in—in their usual state of partial absence of mind, you, on the contrary, perceived every inch of it. As to the length of a bad night, or of a mere time of wakefulness at night, adult words do not measure it; they hardly measure the time of merely waiting for sleep in childhood. Moreover, you were tired of other things, apart from the duration of time—the names of streets, the names of tradesmen, especially the *fournisseurs* of the household, who lived in them.

You were bored by people. It did not occur to you to be tired of those of your own immediate family, for you loved them immemorially. Nor were you bored by the newer personality of casual visitors, unless they held you, as aforesaid, and made you so listen to their unintelligible voices and so look at their mannered faces that they released you an older child than they took you prisoner. But—it is a reluctant confession—you were tired of your relations; you were weary of their bonnets. Measured by adult time, those bonnets were, it is to be presumed, of no more than reasonable duration; they had no more than the average or common life. You have no reason, looking back, to believe that your great-aunts wore bonnets for great and indefinite spaces of time. But, to your sense as a child, long and changing and developing days saw the same harassing artificial flowers hoisted up with the same black lace. You would have had a scruple of conscience as to really disliking the face, but you deliberately let yourself go in detesting the bonnet. So with dresses, especially such as had any little misfit about them. For you it had always existed, and there was no promise of its ceasing. You seemed to have been aware of it for years. By the way, there would be less cheap reproving of little girls for desiring new clothes if the censors knew how immensely old their old clothes are to them.

The fact is that children have a simple sense of the unnecessary ugliness of things, and that—apart from the effects of *ennui*—they reject that ugliness actively. You have stood and listened to your mother's compliments on her friend's hat, and have made your mental protest in very definite words. You thought it hideous, and hideous things offended you then more than they have ever offended you since. At nine years old you made people, alas! responsible for their faces, as you do still in a measure, though you think you do not. You severely made them answer for their clothes, in a manner which you have seen good reason, in later life, to mitigate. Upon curls, or too much youthfulness in the aged, you had no mercy. To sum up the things you hated inordinately, they were friskiness of manner and of trimmings, and curls combined with rather bygone or frumpish fashions. Too much childish dislike was wasted so.

But you admired some things without regard to rules of beauty learnt later. At some seven years old you dwelt with delight upon the contrast of a white kid glove and a bright red wrist. Well, this is not the received arrangement, but red and white do go well together, and their distribution has to be taught with time. Whose were the wrist and glove? Certainly some one's who must have been distressed at the *bouquet* of colour that you admired. This, however, was but a local admiration. You did not admire the girl as a whole. She whom you adored was always a married woman of a certain age; rather faded, it might be, but always divinely elegant. She alone was worthy to stand at the side of your mother. You lay in wait for the border of her train, and dodged for a chance of holding her bracelet when she played. You composed prose in honour of her and called the composition (for reasons unknown to yourself) a "catalogue." She took singularly little notice of you.

Wordsworth cannot say too much of your passion for nature. The light of summer morning before sunrise was to you a spiritual splendour for which you wanted no name. The Mediterranean under the first perceptible touch of the moon, the calm southern sea in the full blossom of summer, the early spring everywhere, in the showery streets, in the fields, or at sea, left old childish memories with you which you try to evoke now when you see them again. But the cloudy dusk behind poplars on the plains of France, the flying landscape from the train, willows, and the last of the light, were more mournful to you then than you care to remember now. So were the black crosses on the graves of the French village; so were cypresses, though greatly beloved.

If you were happy enough to be an internationally educated child, you had much at heart the heart of every country you knew. You disliked the English accent of your compatriots abroad with a scorn to which, needless to say, you are not tempted now. You had shocks of delight from Swiss woods full of lilies of the valley, and from English fields full of cowslips. You had disquieting dreams of landscape and sun, and of many of these you cannot now tell which were visions of travel and which visions of slumber. Your strong sense of place made you love some places too keenly for peace.

www.ingramcontent.com/pod-product-compliance
Lightning Source LLC
LaVergne TN
LVHW041759190726
843493LV00008B/2701